99 Kids Jokes - Stampy Edition Vol 2

JOHN JESTER

Following on from the global success of 99 Kids Jokes – Stampy Edition, Volume 2 has 99 even more hilarious jokes based on Stampy's favourite game for you to enjoy.

Why don't pigs make good minecart drivers?
Why did the snow golem call his wolf Frost?
How did Stampy cure his headache?

Find out the answers to these and many more hysterical jokes. You will never be able to play the game, without laughing out loud, ever again.

1. What letter is part of Stampy's head?

- 'I'!

2. What kind of trees do skeletons like best?

- Ceme-trees!

3. What do zombie villagers put on their hair?

- Scare-spray!

4. What kind of fish do you find in Stampy's bird cage?

- A perch!

5. How do you make a skeleton laugh?

- Tickle its funny bone!

6. What does a wolf say on Halloween?

- Happy HOWLoween!

7. What can't you give a headless guardian?

- A headache!

8. What's the first thing ghasts do when they get in a minecart?

- The boo-kle their seat belts!

9. Where does a zombie villager eat his lunch?

- At the casket-eria!

10. Why did the skeleton play the piano?

- Because he didn't have any organs!

11. Who won the zombie war?

- It was dead even!

12. What kind of bone should you not give to Stampy's pet wolf?

- A trombone!

13. What do you get if you cross a gangster with a hostile mob?

- Organised slime!

14. Why did the cave spider cross the road?

- To prove he wasn't chicken!

15. What do you call a one inch zombie?

- Tomb Thumb!

16. How does Stampy make his tissue dance?

- Puts a little boogie in it!

17. What do you get when you cross a pig and a cactus?

- A porky-pine!

18. What did the zombie say to Stampy at the coffee shop?

- Scream or sugar!

19. Why did the sheep say "moo"?

- It was learning a new language!

20. Why did the chicken cross the road twice?

- Because it was a double crosser!

21. Why did Stampy take a pencil to bed?

- To draw the curtains!

22. How do zombies tell their future?

- With their HORRORscope!

23. What did the skeleton order for dinner?

- Spare ribs!

24. What kind of bird does Stampy use to lift his blocks?

- A crane!

25. How can you carry water in a sieve?

- Make it into an ice block!

26. What did the coal block say to the iron block?

- Nothing. Coal blocks cannot talk!

27. What do ghasts use to clean their hair?

- Sham-boo!

28. Why are spiders good swimmers?

- They have webbed feet!

29. What did Snow White call her chicken?

- Egg white!

30. How do you mend a broken pumpkin?

- With a pumpkin patch!

31. Why did the snow golem call his wolf Frost?

- Because Frost bites!

32. Stampy wanted to marry a ghast.

- I don't know what possessed him!

33. What do you get when you throw a piano down a mine shaft?

- A flat miner!

34. Did you hear the story about Stampy's broken pencil?

- Never mind. It's pointless!

35. How many rotten eggs does it take to make a stink bomb?

- A phew!

36. What do you get if you cross a motorbike with Stampy's joke book?

- A Yamahahaha!

37. Where do boats go when they are feeling ill?

- To the docs!

38. What do you get if you cross Bambi with a ghast?

- Bamboo!

39. What's big, scary, and has three wheels?

- A slime riding a tricycle!

40. What did the doctor say to the skeleton?

- Aren't you a little late?

41. What time do zombies wake up?

- At ate o'clock!

42. Why did Stampy jump up and down before he drank his juice?

- The carton said to shake well before drinking!

43. How do you keep Stampy busy for hours?

- Give him a piece of paper with 'Please turn over' written on both sides!

44. What happened when the cow jumped over the barbed wire?

- It was an udder catastrophe!

45. How do endermen have a bath with no water?

- They sunbathe!

46. Where can you find a zombie eating plants?

- In a vegetarian restaurant!

47. What happened at the blaze's wedding party?

- They toasted the bride and groom!

48. What do wither skeletons put on their bagels?

- Scream cheese!

49. Why did the zombie bring toilet paper to the party?

- Because he was a party pooper!

50. Why does Stampy like to tickle his horse?

- He gets a big kick out of it!

51. Where do pigs go when they lose their tails?

To the retail store!

52. Who won the skeleton beauty contest?

- No body!

53. Where did the ghast go on vacation?

- The BOO-hamas!

54. How did Stampy cure his headache?

- He put his head through a window and the pane just disappeared!

55. What do you say to Stampy driving his minecart with no redstone?

- How's it going?

56. What's red and red and red all over?

- A spotty mooshroom with sunburn!

57. What goes tick, tock, tick, tock, woof?

- Stampy's watchdog!

58. Why don't pigs make good minecart drivers?

- They are road hogs!

59. How do minecarts hear?

- Through their engine-ears!

60. How do zombies travel on holiday?

- On a scare plane!

61. How do you know eating carrots is good for your eyes?

- Have you ever seen a rabbit wearing spectacles?

62. Who brings a zombie's baby?

- Franken-stork!

63. Why is the letter K like a pig's tail?

- Because it's the end of Pork!

64. When you take away 2 letters from this 5-letter word, you are left with 1. What is it?

- Stone!

65. What follows a skeleton horse wherever he goes?

- His tail of course!

66. Why did the one-handed pig farmer cross the road?

- To get to the second-hand shop!

67. If twenty endermen chase Stampy, what time is it?

- Twenty after one!

68. What does a zombie villager eat with cheese?

- Pickled organs!

69. Where do ghasts go when they want a swim?

- The dead sea!

70. What do you call a haunted chicken?

- A poultry-geist!

71. What's the best way to talk to a spider jockey?

- From afar!

72. What is a ghast's favourite dessert?

- Boo-berry pie!

73. Where should a 500 pound silverfish go?

- On a diet!

74. What should you do with a green slime?

- Wait until its ripe!

75. What is the radius of a pumpkin?

- Pi!

76. What do you get when two skeletons dance in a chest?

- Noise!

77. What is worse than being a three hundred pound spider jockey?

- Being the spider!

78. What is a ghast's favourite party game?

- Hide and shriek!

79. What are spiders webs good for?

- Spiders!

80. What do you call two young married spiders?

- Newly webs!

81. What kind of horses do ghasts like to ride?

- Night-mares!

82. What medicine do zombie villagers take for colds?

- Coffin drops!

83. Why did the minecart stop when it saw a ghast?

- It had a nervous breakdown!

84. How does Stampy count his cows?

- With a Cow-culator!

85. What is invisible and smells like carrots?

- A rabbit fart!

86. Do zombies eat pumpkins with their fingers?

- No, they eat the fingers separately!

87. The past, present and future walk into Stampy's house.

- It was tense!

88. How are zombie villagers like computers?

- They use megaBITES!

89. What do you call a cow with a twitch?

- Beef jerky!

90. Why did Stampy take a ruler to bed?

- He wanted to see how long he slept!

91. Where do zombies go on cruises?

- The DEADiterranean Sea!

92. Stampy walked into a bar.

- Ouch!

93. Why was Stampy staring so hard at his orange juice?

- Because the carton said concentrate.

94. Why does Stampy always walk with his right foot first?

- Because when he puts one foot forward the other is left behind!

95. What do you call a song sung in a minecart?

- A cartoon (car tune)!

96. What do you get when you cross a cement mixer and a chicken?

- A brick layer!

97. Stampy, Amy Lee and L'for lee are stranded in the End and find a genie lamp. The genie grants them each one wish. Amy Lee wishes she was back home, and poof, she is back home. L'for lee wishes the same thing, and poof, he is back home. Stampy, feeling lonely, has his wish. "I'm lonely. Can I have my friends back?"

98. Why did Stampy want a job at the bakery?

- So he could loaf around!

99. What did the mommy ghast say to the baby ghast?

- Don't spook until you're spoken to!